Richard's Visits to Leicester

Richard III (1452–85) reigned for only two years and two months, from June 1483 to August 1485, but the suspicion that he murdered his nephews, the 'Princes in the Tower', coupled with Shakespeare's brilliant character assassination has made him easily the most notorious – and controversial – of English monarchs. Time did not allow him to see all parts of his kingdom, but he was familiar with Leicester, which he visited on at least four occasions between 1483 and 1484. He stayed at the castle from 17–20 August 1483 in the course of his post-coronation 'progress', or tour of England, and was back on 22–23 October mustering troops to oppose the rebellion of his former ally, the Duke of Buckingham. On 31 July 1484 he spent a night

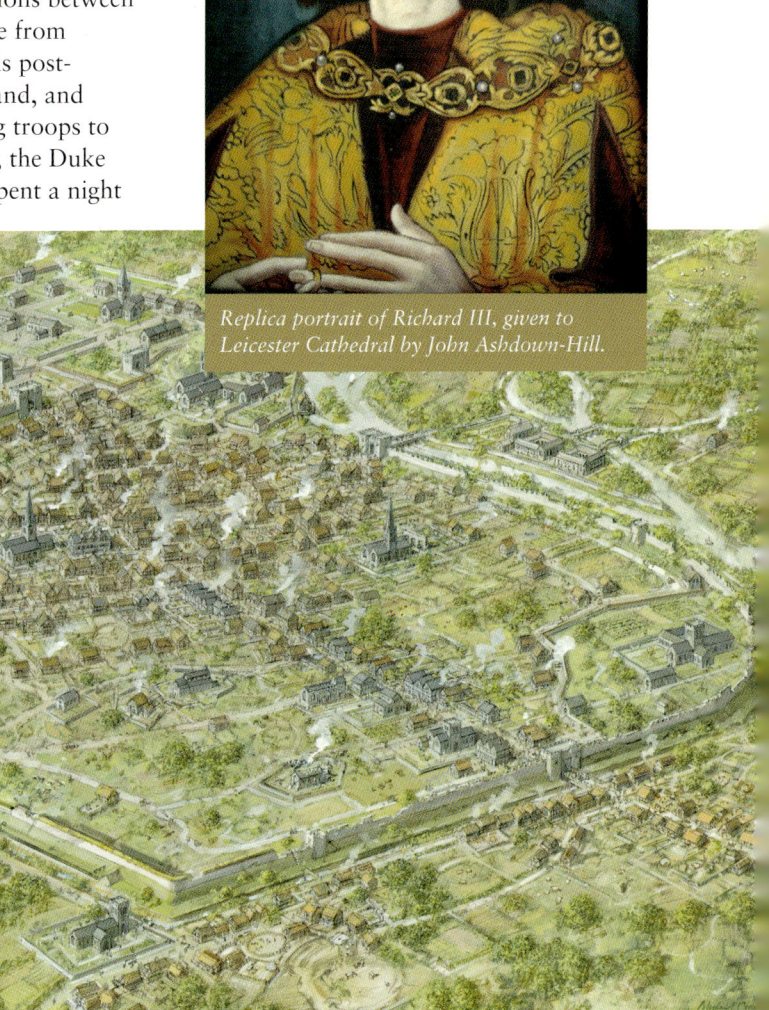

Replica portrait of Richard III, given to Leicester Cathedral by John Ashdown-Hill.

A watercolour by Mike Codd depicting a 15th-century view of East Leicester, Leicester Cathedral and Grey Friars as Richard III might have known them.

John Fulleylove's painting of 1880 illustrates the continuing impact of the King's story and connections with the city of Leicester.

The Turret Gateway at Leicester Castle.

at St Mary's Abbey, beyond the north wall, while travelling from Nottingham to Westminster, and broke a similar journey either there or in the town on 5 November. We know of these visits because Richard happened to issue an order or sign a document, but there could be others that passed unrecorded or unremarked.

Leicester had long been a stronghold of the vanquished House of Lancaster, and so the Yorkist Richard wanted to establish a good relationship with the townsfolk. The abbot of St Mary's was given permission to hold an annual fair in the abbey and in the parish of St Leonard for two days before the saint's feast day and for two afterwards; and when the dean and canons of the collegiate church in the Newarke complained that royal officials were withholding the revenues of some Welsh lands that formed part of their endowment, Richard authorised them to appoint a representative to visit the area, ascertain how much was owed, and enforce payment. Local men who had offended against the King's laws were pardoned, and on 24 November 1484 Richard – 'in consideration of the true and faithful service which our well-beloved Mayor and burgesses of our town of Leicester have rendered to us, as also in relief of their costs had and borne in this behalf, as also of the great ruin and decay in which the aforesaid town now is' – granted them an annuity of £20 for 20 years.

Local Myths and Legends

There are several stories about Richard's time in the city that have passed into local legend. Leicester's central location made it an ideal place to assemble forces to resist threats from all parts of the country, and Richard used it as a rallying point when Henry Tudor's invading army approached the Midlands in August 1485. He arrived on either Friday 19 or Saturday 20 August and, according to tradition, lodged at the White Boar Inn in High Street, the modern Highcross Street. The name of the inn was allegedly changed to the *Blue* Boar (a badge of the Lancastrian Earl of Oxford) in the aftermath of the battle of Bosworth, and the travelling bedstead Richard is said to have left there is now displayed at Donington-le-Heath Manor House, near Coalville in north-west Leicestershire. There is a story that a later landlady, a Mrs Clark,

The Blue Boar Inn, originally called the White Boar Inn.

Richard III's bed, on display at Donington-le-Heath Manor House. The house and gardens are open to the public.

found a large amount of money concealed in it and was murdered for her wealth in James I's reign. She was certainly killed and her attackers condemned and executed: but the King's bed was not mentioned at their trial and there is reason to believe that her riches owed more to hard work than to luck.

Richard marshalled his army in the town on the morning of Sunday 21 August and marched out over Bow Bridge, in the words of a contemporary, 'with great triumph and pomp'. Sir Richard Baker wrote in about 1625 that 'upon this bridge stood a stone of some height; against which King Richard, as he passed toward Bosworth, by chance struck his spur: and against the same stone, as he was brought back, hanging by the horse-side, his head was dashed and broken: as a

RICHARD III

Left: Locals enjoy a Richard III coronation pageant in Leicester in 1911.

Below: The myth that the body of the King was disinterred at the time of the Dissolution and thrown into the River Soar, under Bow Bridge, was mentioned by John Speed 'as tradition hath delivered' in 1611. The legend continued to grow until this plaque was erected on Bow Bridge in 1856. It now carries a disclaimer, erected by the Richard III Society.

wise woman (forsooth) had foretold: who before his going to battle, being asked of his success, said, that where his spur struck, his head should be broken.' Baker makes it clear that he was only reporting hearsay however, and so was John Nichols, the historian of Leicester, who noted another story included in a work entitled *Ten Strange Prophecies* published in 1644. According to this:

'... as King Richard the Third, before the battle of Bosworth, rode through the south [sic] gate of Leicester; a poor old blind man (by profession a wheelwright) sat begging, and, hearing his approach, said, that if the Moon changed twice that day, having by her ordinary course changed in the morning, King Richard should lose his crown, and be slain. And a nobleman that carried the Moon for his colours revolted; thereby he lost his life and kingdom.'

The moon and the nobleman in question are not readily identifiable, but Lord Thomas Stanley's arms incorporated three plates argent (silver or white discs), which could be taken for full moons, while those of his brother Sir William were differenced by a crescent (moon) indicating that he was a second son. Their disloyalty undoubtedly contributed to Richard's downfall, but again, it may be a case of someone being wise after the event.

The original Bow Bridge was demolished in 1861 but its replacement was designed by the city as a memorial to Richard III, its ironwork depicting the white rose of York, the Tudor rose of Lancaster, Richard's white boar emblem and his motto 'Loyaulte me Lie' (Loyalty Binds Me).

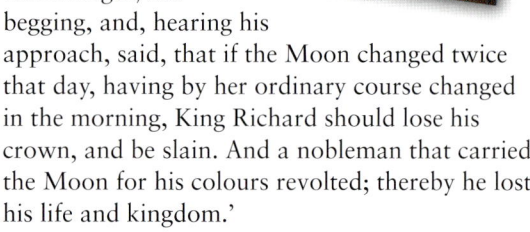

Leicester in 1485

The Blue Boar Inn was demolished in 1836 and Bow Bridge rebuilt in 1861, but drawings exist showing how both might have appeared in Richard's day. Much of late medieval Leicester has disappeared with the passing of the centuries, but there are still a number of buildings the King would have recognised. He would surely have been impressed by the Norman Great Hall of the castle, 'the oldest surviving aisled and bay-divided hall in Europe', which he would have seen before it acquired its late 17th-century brick frontage and before panelling obscured the interior. He almost certainly worshipped in the castle church of St Mary 'de Castro', and would have at least noticed the four other surviving medieval churches: All Saints (which he would have passed as he rode into Leicester from Nottingham), St Margaret's, St Martin's (now the cathedral) and St Nicholas. Some of their fabric has since been restored, but among the more notable surviving medieval features are the Norman sedilia in the chancel of St Mary 'de Castro'; the tower of St Nicholas, which incorporates courses of herringbone masonry formed by Roman tiles; the unusual projecting, perhaps once detached, tower of All Saints; and the rare 15th-century oak-vaulted roof with fan tracery in the north porch of St Martin's. Little remains of St Mary's Abbey, but the alabaster tomb of Richard's contemporary John Penny, who was abbot from 1496 to 1508, is preserved in St Margaret's church.

If Richard took the short walk from the castle through the Turret Gateway he would have entered the Newarke, the complex of buildings founded and extended by Henry Earl

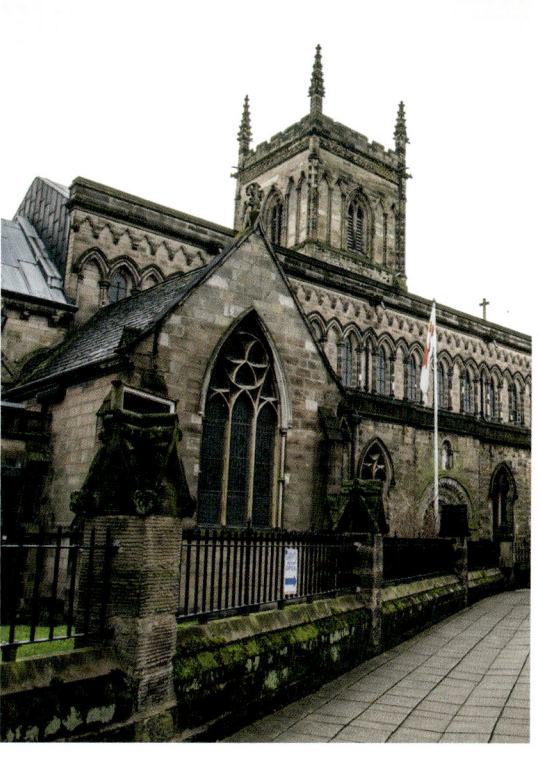

The Great Hall at Leicester Castle.

St Mary 'de Castro' Church from Castle Yard.

Left: The 'Magazine' Gateway in the Newarke.

Below left: The interior of the 'Magazine' Gateway in the Newarke.

begun in 1536. If Henry VIII's plan to create 13 new dioceses had been brought to fruition it would have become the cathedral of a re-founded diocese of Leicester, but instead it lay in ruins by 1590. Richard could not have foreseen that his naked body would be displayed there in the aftermath of the Battle of Bosworth, a gesture designed to scotch rumours that he had somehow survived the conflict. Two restored arches in De Montfort University's Hawthorn Building are all that remain of the church today.

of Lancaster and his son Henry, the first Duke of that title, in the middle of the 14th century. He would have noted the Newarke or 'Magazine' Gateway, which gave access to the southern part of the town; the 'hospital', or alms house, with its chapel (preserved in Trinity House); and, most magnificent of all, the collegiate church of the Annunciation of St Mary in the Newarke completed only half a century earlier. In Richard's time it contained the tombs of the founders together with those of other members of the Lancastrian royal family and many local worthies, but it failed to survive the Dissolution of the religious establishments

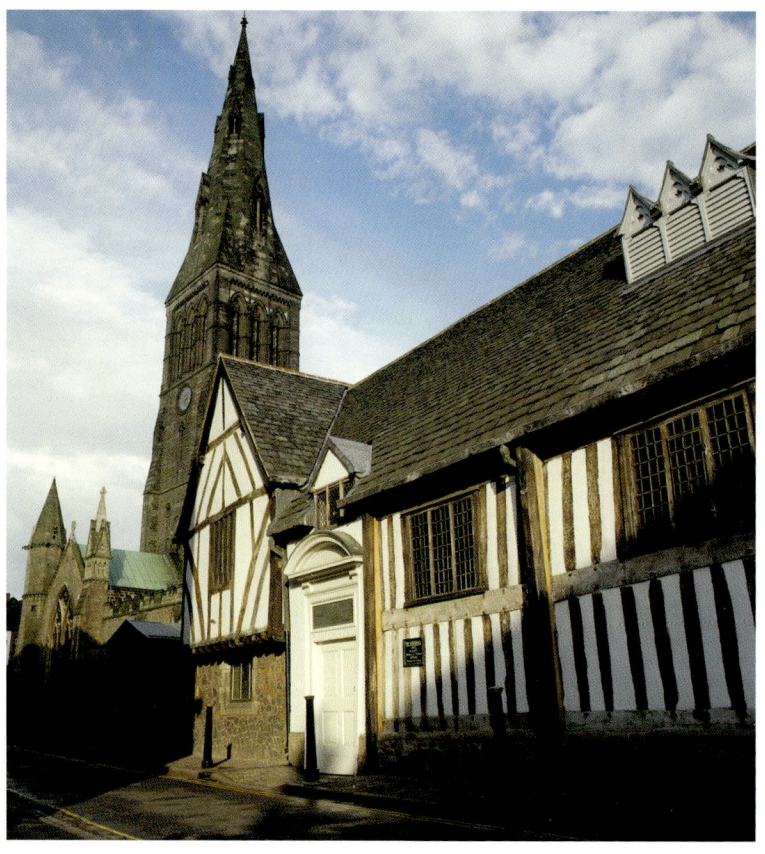

The Guildhall, built around 1390, and Leicester Cathedral behind.

The Battle of Bosworth

On the morning of 22 August 1485, Richard's large royal army and Henry Tudor's smaller rebel force faced each other near the villages of Stoke Golding and Dadlington in south-west Leicestershire. At first Richard seemed to have the advantage, but he was outmanoeuvred by Henry's military commander, his rearguard failed to engage the enemy, and other supporters changed sides. Richard tried to seize the initiative by charging across the battlefield to confront Henry, but was overwhelmed 'fighting manfully in the thickest presse of his enemyes'. He became the last English king to die in battle and the first since 1066.

Before 2010 the exact location of the battle was the subject of much debate; until survey work and extensive historical research (commissioned by Bosworth Battlefield Heritage Centre and funded by the Heritage Lottery Fund) found the largest collection of round shot on a European medieval battlefield. Silver coins, fragments of military and clothing, fittings and horse harness pendants were also unearthed.

This iconic silver-gilt boar badge, worn by one of Richard's high-ranking supporters, was found immediately adjacent to an area of proven medieval marshland, likely to be the marsh mentioned by chroniclers of the battle and later made famous by Shakespeare.

The Battle of Bosworth: a detail from a 1610 engraving by John Speed.

Richard's Burial in Leicester

After two days of public humiliation Richard was hurriedly buried in the church of the Franciscan (Grey) friars in a grave that was too small for even his slight frame to lie in. Decomposition may have made haste essential, but it is also possible that those charged with making the cutting simply misjudged the King's height. According to Polydore Vergil, Henry VII's court historian, he was laid to rest 'without any pomp or solemn funeral', but this should not be taken to mean that the friars failed to perform the appropriate religious rites or to pray for his soul.

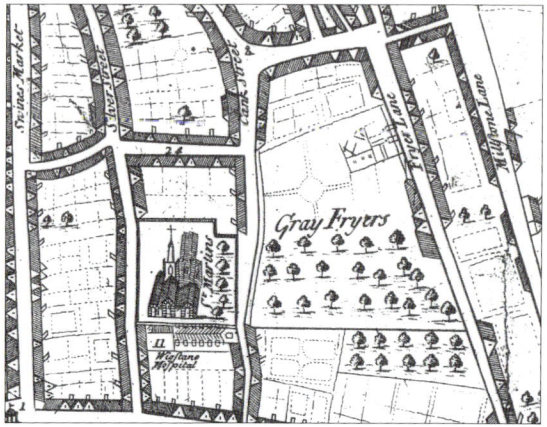

A 1741 map of 'Gray Fryers' by Thomas Roberts. It was here that Richard III was buried following his death on the battlefield at Bosworth.

Ten years later, King Henry paid for a memorial in the form of a box tomb to be erected above the grave of his late rival, but this did not long survive the suppression of the friary in 1538. The place of the King's burial was still remembered when Alderman Robert Herrick, who had bought the site and built a house on part of it, erected a small stone pillar bearing the legend 'Here lies the Body of Richard III, some Time King of England' around 1600 in what was then his garden; but this, too, vanished, perhaps in the battles fought in Leicester at the end of the English Civil War. It was probably after this that the legend that the King's bones had been exhumed and thrown into the river became popular, and later visitors to the town allowed their attention to be diverted to a stone coffin being used as a horse trough, which they were wrongly told had once contained Richard's body. Herrick's house was demolished in 1870 and there was further redevelopment: but the site was not entirely built over and the open space became a Council car park in later years.

T.C. Barfield's 1927 painting shows Richard III outside the White Boar Inn, on his way to battle.

Richard Re-Discovered

In late 2010 Philippa Langley approached Leicester City Council with a proposal that the car park where part of Alderman Herrick's garden and the Franciscan friary had once stood should be investigated. A team of archaeologists led by Richard Buckley undertook an assessment and developed an excavation strategy to explore the site; and the dig, jointly funded by the Council, the University of Leicester and the Richard III Society, commenced on Saturday 25 August 2012. The omens were not promising. A survey using ground-penetrating radar undertaken the previous year had failed to identify recognisable walls, and few thought it would be possible to find the king's body. Remarkably, however, human bones that would subsequently be identified as Richard's were located on the very first day of the dig.

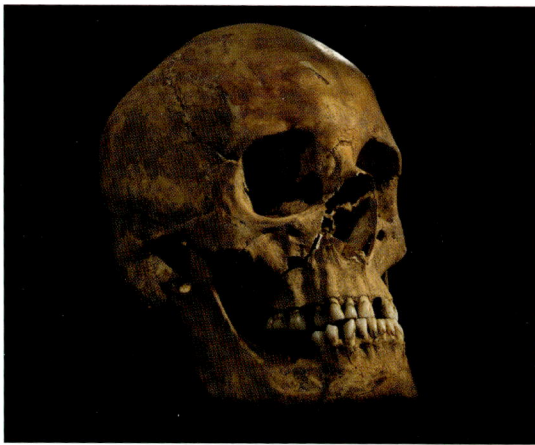

Richard III's skull: maxilla wound.

Skeletal and dental evidence indicated that these were the remains of a man who had died in his early 30s (Richard was nearly 33 when he was killed at Bosworth), and of a markedly slender build. His natural height was five feet eight inches, a little taller than average, but scoliosis (curvature of the spine) would have reduced this by some inches and raised his right shoulder higher than his left. He was not a hunchback, however – the curvature was lateral, or sideways – and there was nothing to substantiate Sir Thomas More's claim that Richard also had a withered arm. Indeed, the physical disfigurement was probably slight. Richard's torso would have been short relative to the length of his limbs, but a good tailor and custom-made armour could have minimised the visual impact.

The victim suffered two fatal blows to the back of the head inflicted by bladed weapons: one was a penetrating wound and the other cut away part of the base of his skull. There were nine other, lesser wounds to both the head and torso including some, described as 'insult injuries', apparently inflicted after death when the body had been stripped of armour. Even King Richard's

The skeleton in situ.

enemies did not deny that he had died fighting bravely; and while the remains *could* have been those of another slightly built person who suffered from scoliosis and who had been buried in the Franciscan friary after experiencing considerable trauma, there was every reason to conclude that they were his.

If the skeleton had been found a generation ago, not much more information could have been obtained from it: but today, high-precision radiocarbon dating can pinpoint the age of the remains to within 70 years; stable isotope analysis can help establish the individual's lifestyle, environment and diet (by identifying

Open Day at the Richard III dig site in 2012.

the geological origin of the minerals his teeth had absorbed from food and drink during their formation); and genetic analysis can match his DNA to another member of his family.

Radiocarbon dating has demonstrated that the individual, who lived between 1450 and 1540, enjoyed a high-protein diet and was therefore of high status.

Richard III left no living descendants but individuals related to Richard through either an all-female or all-male line would be expected to share an identical or near-identical mitochondrial DNA or Y chromosome type respectively.

After Dr John Ashdown-Hill had built upon earlier work and importantly identified the Ibsen family as being female-line relatives of Richard III, Professor Kevin Schürer set out to confirm their family link with Richard III through Anne of York and find another individual who could act as a comparator. The Professor and his team confirmed the lineage through Richard's eldest sister, demonstrating that Wendy Duldig and Michael Ibsen are 14th cousins twice removed from one another through the female line. Both agreed to give a DNA sample so Dr Turi King, who was leading the genetic analysis in the case, could compare their mitochondrial DNA with that from the skeletal remains. Mitochondrial DNA analysis showed a perfect match between the skeleton and Michael Ibsen, and a single difference (a mutation which is not unexpected) with Wendy Duldig. Furthermore, this mitochondrial DNA type was shown to be very rare. The Y chromosome analysis did not

DNA (deoxyribonucleic acid)

The genetic analysis compares the DNA of an individual with that of a known relative. However, not just any relative could act as a comparator for these remains as the vast majority of our DNA is a highly complex mixture of DNA inherited from ancestors and cannot be used for DNA identification purposes. However, two segments of our DNA are inherited simply through the generations virtually unchanged, save for the gradual accumulation of little mutations:

- Mitochondrial DNA is passed down by a mother to all of her children, but only daughters can pass it on.
- The Y chromosome causes an embryo to develop as a boy and so can only be passed down from father to son.

show a match and indicated that at least two false paternities (where the father is not the recorded father) must have occurred: one recently and one in the 19 generations which separate Richard III from Henry Somerset (see diagram).

A statistical analysis of the combined genetic and non-genetic evidence showed that, even at its most conservative, the probability of the remains being those of Richard III is some 99.999%.

There are no contemporary portraits of Richard III, so Dr King was interested in genetically determining his hair and eye colour. The DNA analysis showed that he almost certainly had blue eyes and there was a high probability that his hair was blond – at least during his childhood. His hair could have darkened with age. Based on this, it is suggested that the best likeness is the arched-frame portrait owned by the Society of Antiquaries of London.

Family Tree Showing the Female Line

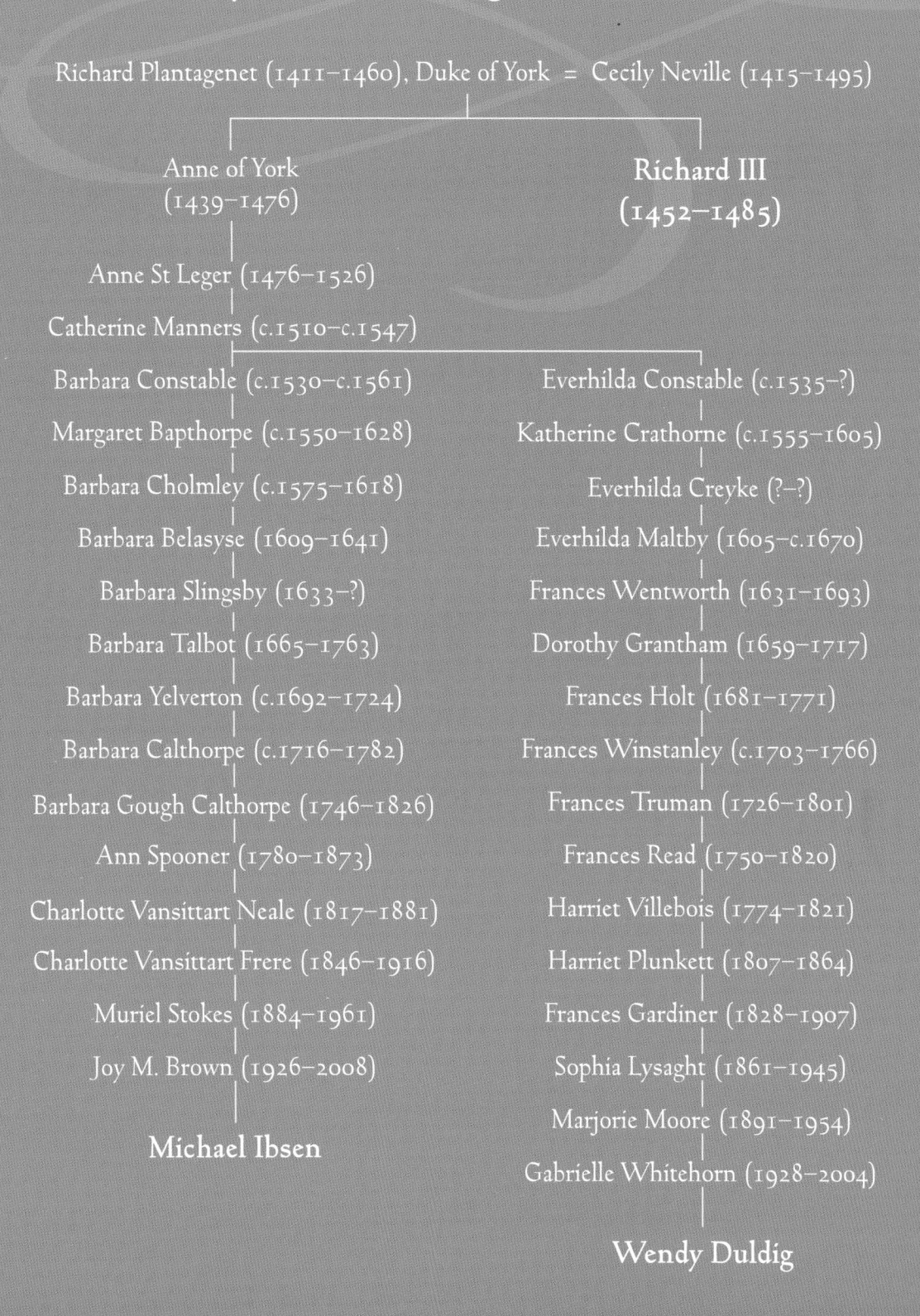

Richard Plantagenet (1411–1460), Duke of York = Cecily Neville (1415–1495)

Anne of York (1439–1476) | Richard III (1452–1485)

Anne St Leger (1476–1526)
Catherine Manners (c.1510–c.1547)

Female line to Michael Ibsen	Female line to Wendy Duldig
Barbara Constable (c.1530–c.1561)	Everhilda Constable (c.1535–?)
Margaret Bapthorpe (c.1550–1628)	Katherine Crathorne (c.1555–1605)
Barbara Cholmley (c.1575–1618)	Everhilda Creyke (?–?)
Barbara Belasyse (1609–1641)	Everhilda Maltby (1605–c.1670)
Barbara Slingsby (1633–?)	Frances Wentworth (1631–1693)
Barbara Talbot (1665–1763)	Dorothy Grantham (1659–1717)
Barbara Yelverton (c.1692–1724)	Frances Holt (1681–1771)
Barbara Calthorpe (c.1716–1782)	Frances Winstanley (c.1703–1766)
Barbara Gough Calthorpe (1746–1826)	Frances Truman (1726–1801)
Ann Spooner (1780–1873)	Frances Read (1750–1820)
Charlotte Vansittart Neale (1817–1881)	Harriet Villebois (1774–1821)
Charlotte Vansittart Frere (1846–1916)	Harriet Plunkett (1807–1864)
Muriel Stokes (1884–1961)	Frances Gardiner (1828–1907)
Joy M. Brown (1926–2008)	Sophia Lysaght (1861–1945)
	Marjorie Moore (1891–1954)
	Gabrielle Whitehorn (1928–2004)
Michael Ibsen	**Wendy Duldig**

King Richard III Visitor Centre

Far left: The courtyard at the King Richard III Visitor Centre.

Left: The entrance to the King Richard III Visitor Centre.

Less than two years passed between Leicester City Council purchasing an old school building with the aim of creating a centre that would tell the story of the remarkable search for, and discovery of, King Richard III, and the Visitor Centre's opening day.

The former Alderman Newton's School, located next to the spot where the King's remains were found, was transformed, and the King Richard III Visitor Centre opened its doors to the public on 26 July 2014.

Using captivating storytelling, beautiful design and 21st-century technology, the Visitor Centre tells the fascinating and moving story of the King's life and death, and reveals one of the greatest archaeological detective stories ever told.

This unique story is told in three parts:

Dynasty puts visitors at the heart of medieval England, racked by decades of turbulence and fighting during the Wars of the Roses. Here they can discover the much-debated story behind Richard's rise to power as the last king from the great house of Plantagenet and the reforms he introduced during his short reign.

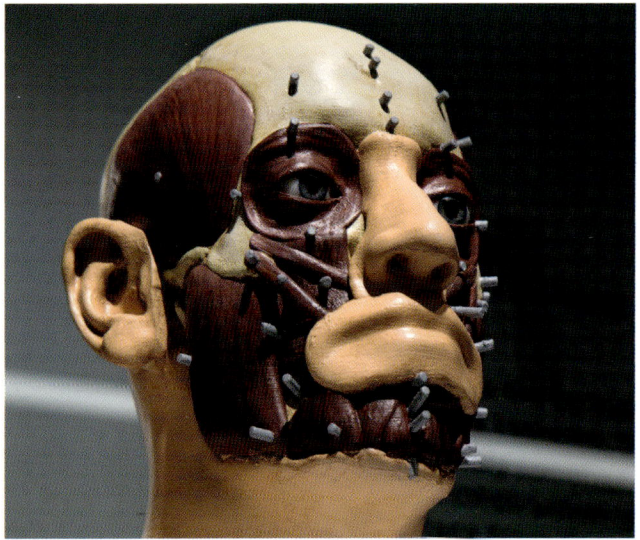

The facial reconstruction of King Richard III.

The site of King Richard III's burial.

A recreation of the Battle of Bosworth.

Death is where the thunder of hooves and the rallying war cries can be heard as visitors are transported back to the Battle of Bosworth. Find out how betrayal led to the King being cut down in the thick of battle while defending his crown, and his return to Leicester.

Discovery unearths the astonishing story of the research, archaeology, science and analysis carried out to discover and identify the long-lost remains of the King. Visitors can see both a partial and the full facial reconstruction, and there is also a replica of Richard's skeleton, printed using 3D technology. The skeleton clearly shows his curved spine, as well as his battle injuries including the fatal blows.

Visitors then return to the ground floor to complete their experience with a visit to the site of King Richard's burial, preserved in a quiet, respectful setting with a contemplative atmosphere, fitting for the last resting place of a slain warrior and anointed monarch.

The throne room.

The Final Journey of King Richard III

King Richard's final journey through Leicestershire began at Fenn Lane Farm, Upton, which is located within what is known to be Bosworth Battlefield. The area is overlooked by Crown Hill, Stoke Golding, where the victorious Henry Tudor was unofficially crowned after the battle.

After a private ceremony on the battlefield, King Richard's coffin was taken to the nearby village of Dadlington, where many of those who fell in the battle were buried. In 1513 King Henry VIII authorised the churchwardens to collect money to fund the building of a chantry chapel in which priests would pray for the victims' souls.

The cortege then paused in the village of Sutton Cheney, where Richard is reputed to have heard Mass in St James' Church the night before the battle.

The next stop was Ambion Hill, where the 16th-century historian Raphael Holinshed said that Richard 'pitched his field' before the battle. The hill is home to Bosworth Battlefield Heritage Centre, and a service of remembrance and reconciliation was held by the Bishop of Leicester, the Rt Reverend Tim Stevens, at the Memorial Sundial which commemorates those who fell in the battle while overlooking the battlefield itself.

The Memorial Sundial at the Bosworth Battlefield Heritage Centre.

King Richard's cortege then passed through Market Bosworth, which, as the nearest substantial town, gave its name to the battle, and then on through Newbold Verdon, Desford and Leicester Forest East. After being received at Bow Bridge, Leicester, it arrived at the King's final resting place in Leicester Cathedral.

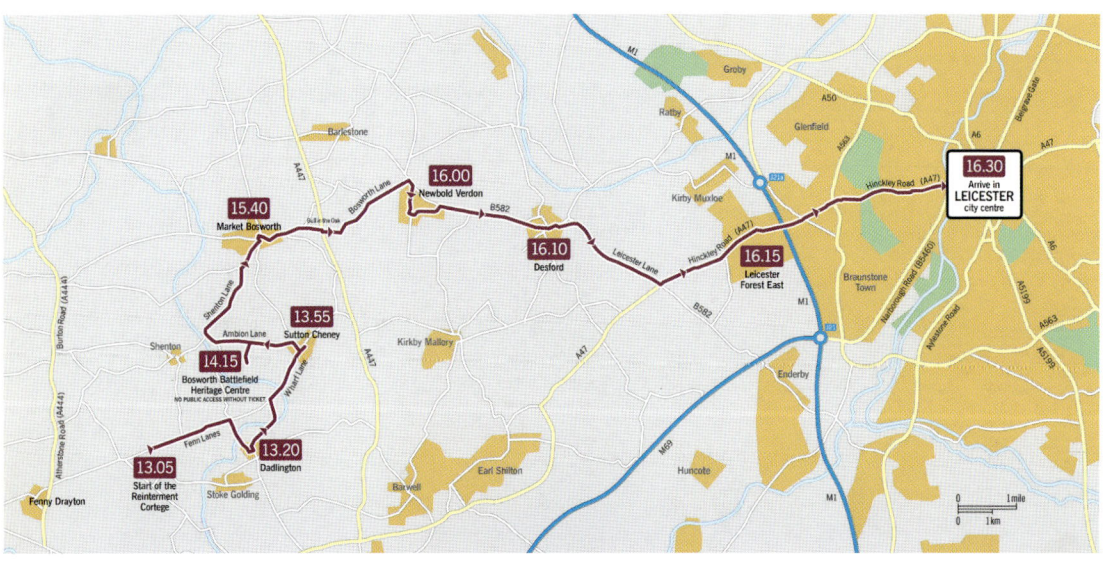

Reinterment in Leicester Cathedral

In response to an application for judicial review, the High Court ruled in May 2014 that the mortal remains of King Richard III should be reinterred in Leicester Cathedral, all due legal process having been properly followed during the exhumation. Located next to the medieval Guildhall, St Martin's was already the most significant parish church in the city and became the cathedral in 1927 on the formation of the modern diocese of Leicester. The cathedral is also situated very close to where Grey Friars church once stood, and where the grave and remains of Richard III were discovered. This is now the site of the new King Richard III Visitor Centre.

View of the ambulatory and King Richard III's tomb. Image courtesy of van Heyningen and Haward Architects.

The cathedral has been reordered specifically to create a space within the chancel for the tomb of King Richard III. Replacement liturgical furnishings, a striking new altar and cathedra (bishop's seat) were created to complement these arrangements.

Richard's story of discovery and reinterment belongs as much to the 21st century as it does to the 15th. That is why his tomb, designed by James McCosh of van Heyningen and Haward Architects, is not a medieval pastiche but explicitly designed to reflect the time in which the king was reinterred. The coffin itself is below ground in a vault, beneath a large shaped block of Swaledale fossil stone deeply incised with a cross. This in turn sits on a dark plinth of Kilkenny limestone, carved with King Richard's name, dates, motto and royal coat of arms. The tomb can be found within an ambulatory, created between the newly designated Chapel of Christ the King at the east end of the cathedral and the new sanctuary in the crossing under the tower.

The model of King Richard III's tomb overhead from the east. Image courtesy of van Heyningen and Haward Architects.

Leicester Cathedral.

It is tilted eastwards, as if facing the Lord coming at the last day, and depicted as such in the great east window. It is designed so light flows through the deep-cut cross, symbolising the Christian faith of hope even in the face of death. There are plans to install two stained-glass windows in the adjacent Chapel of St Katharine, to be created by the renowned artist Tom Denny, relating the story of the last of the medieval Kings of England to the experience of the modern pilgrim.

On 22 March 2015 the University of Leicester transferred Richard's mortal remains into a lead-lined coffin, made from English oak by his known descendant Michael Ibsen, a carpenter. King Richard's remains completed their final journey through the city in a horse-drawn carriage and, on reaching Leicester Cathedral in the early evening, were transferred to the care of the Church during an evening service of Compline, at which the Catholic Archbishop of Westminster, Cardinal Vincent Nichols, preached the sermon.

For three days King Richard's remains then lay in repose, the coffin covered with an embroidered pall showing mourners from his time and also key figures in the story of rediscovery. Special arrangements were in place to allow as many as possible to pay their respects and say their prayers. The reburial service took place on 26 March, led by the Archbishop of Canterbury, the Most Reverend Justin Welby, so bringing to an end the remarkable journey of the last Plantagenet King. Overnight the two-ton stone topping of the grave was put in place, and at a special service the following day the tomb was revealed for the first time in its final and lasting position.

Richard is as controversial now as he ever was, and therein lies the continuing fascination with him. We must hope that future research will shed as much light on his character and actions as science has done on his physical being, and that this most remarkable discovery, which has caught the world's imagination, will foster an interest in Plantagenet history far into the future. We also hope that visitors will continue to be drawn to Leicester, the city which has been so closely associated with him for so many centuries.